HOW TO GET THE MOST OUT OF LIFE

Books by Ernest L. Ramer

How to Get the Most Out of Life
Religion Through Reason
The Catholic Church of the Future

How to Get the Most Out of Life

Ernest L. Ramer

Exposition Press   Hicksville, New York

FIRST EDITION

© 1975 by Ernest L. Ramer

ISBN 0-682-48292-7

Printed in the United States of America

DEDICATION

This book was made possible by the help of my brother, Leonard V. Ramer, who gave me the understanding that all people belong to God and every person has human weaknesses; also, that good can be found in each person. He believed that we should try to see the good in others and overlook their human faults.

Leonard has now passed on to receive his everlasting reward from Christ and God.

Contents

Introduction

How should a person live his life on earth? This is a question of greatest importance to each one of us.

Did God our creator have any definite plan for the billions of people who have been born and live on earth through his supernatural power?

There just isn't any limit to the variety of God's creatures, nor is there any limit to number as far as we as human beings can understand. The extent of the universe, with all of its stars and planets, is beyond the imagination of people. The important point to remember is that the human race is just one of the unlimited numbers of God's creations.

It is not hard to realize that God is the master and controlling force of the complete universe and all of his creations.

God does have a very definite purpose in the creation of everything he has made. He has made little creatures so small we can't even see them. Perhaps with a microscope we can look at them. We don't know why God wanted them, but he did.

We certainly can see that every one of God's creatures is important to him in one way or another. Therefore, every human being is important to God, because each one of us represents a creature with intelligence and the ability to do many different things.

Also, God has built into human beings something that is supernatural and capable of life after our bodies have lived and died on earth. Through Christ, his only son, God has let people know there can be supernatural life for each one of us with God after our earthly death, if that is what we sincerely want. That is the way people can be with God and enjoy the same way of life that God enjoys. Certainly, there can be nothing but true happiness with God and his people who have lived their lives on earth and have already joined him in Heaven.

With the billions of people here on earth, there is no doubt that God has a very definite plan which he wants his people to follow during their life on earth.

There are a great number of people born every day, and a great number who die every day. Thus, there is a continuous exchange of people on earth.

Whatever change comes with the death of our bodies, there must be a place for us to go, as supernatural beings, to be with God, or to be some other place without him.

The determining factor is the ability God has given people to choose the way they want to live while they are on earth.

A reward for living according to God just cannot be forced on people. A reward is received after we have earned it. That is true in everyday living on earth.

If God forced us to do what he wanted, then there would have been no reason for him to go to all the work of creating the world and everything in it. We would have no choice of our own between what we want or what God wants. We could not decide for ourselves. A reward would be automatic; we would not have to earn it.

People find themselves with a freedom of choice as to whether they want to follow God or not. That is entirely up to them. The only exceptions are the people who are deficient and cannot reason. Since they are not able to decide for themselves, God must give them his reward without their earning it.

God has made it easily understood that we all have to die sooner or later, so we all know he has complete control of human beings in the final end.

God takes over in determining our existence as human beings after death. He is the absolute power; we have no choice at that time. We have already had our chance to choose while living on earth.

The way we choose to live is our own individual problem. Each one of us is responsible to God for our life only. We are not responsible for other people, or the way they choose to live.

HOW TO GET THE MOST OUT OF LIFE

God's Purpose
In Creating the World

HOW TO GET THE MOST OUT OF LIFE

The earth is a planet very great in size. It is about 25,000 miles around the earth. Think of the many continents and the vast size of most of them. Consider the land, the lakes, the rivers, the mountains, the oceans, the forests, the deserts and many other features in the makeup of the earth. Then there are thousands of different types of living creatures on the earth today, including billions of human beings.

It is beyond human comprehension to understand all the work God has performed from the beginning of the earth's creation, probably several billion years ago, until now.

The number of different living creatures that have come and gone millions of years ago will never be known.

All through these billions of years God has created the forces that changed the world from one period to another until we find the world as it is today.

The supernatural power of God is displayed first in the development of the earth and all the rest of the universe and, even more important, in the control and regulation of everything to maintain perfect order in the operation of the universe.

Why did God create the world with all of its living creatures? Such a fantastic development certainly was not without any definite purpose.

Our very existence here on earth proves that God wanted the earth for people to live on.

Next God developed other necessities such as water, soil to grow the things we need to maintain life, trees, fruits, vegetables, animals, and everything else we need.

Imagine what a supernatural force it takes to maintain the conditions that make it possible for people to live and continue to populate the world from generation to generation. Probably, people have existed on earth fifty thousand years or longer—beginning with early man.

The history of the earth and its inhabitants is fascinating. Some people spend their lifetime trying to dig into the earth and uncover the remains of thousands, millions, and even billions of years ago. What were these prehistoric creatures like? It is most interesting to study prehistoric life.

When we think of these works of God, we realize that he certainly had a very definite plan in creating the world and also a very definite reason for creating every person who ever has or ever will live on this earth.

With this fantastic world in which each one of us finds himself existing as a human being, we can very definitely understand that God has given us a wonderful place to live during our brief lifetimes. Certainly, there is a vast difference in the lifespan of the average human being as compared with the millions or billions of years the earth has existed. So our short trip here on earth is just the beginning for each person.

Our conclusion is that God created the world for one very important reason: a place for you and me to be born, to live, and to die.

God's Reason
for People on Earth

Does God want people here on earth to take care of his countless creations besides human beings?

That could have been a reason for God having allowed so many people to be born, living here at this time and in the past.

But we just can't look around and find people being caretakers of God's million or more creatures, plant life, and even the land itself.

As a result, God did not create these things to be taken care of by his human beings. So there must be other reasons for people existing on earth.

Did God want people to exist on earth so they could gradually, from generation to generation, improve the living conditions, so over the centuries it would be easier for people to make their way through life? Also, would the abilities of people make it possible for human beings to live longer on earth?

The creation of the human race certainly proves God's ability to create people with tremendous possibilities of accomplishments. The achievements of people seem to come within the realm of personal accomplishments that enhance the lives of individuals rather than work they might be doing for God.

Thus it can be understood that we are working for ourselves instead of helping God with his job of maintaining the earth with all of its creatures.

17

We can readily understand that God has not made the billions of people just to populate the earth and live here indefinitely, enjoying the pleasures from both nature and man-made activities.

We have no other choice than to believe that God had a very important reason to populate the earth with people, let them live here a few years at the most, and then apparently let them die. Some babies die even before they are born. Certainly, with this kind of a plan, God must have a program for people after their death on this earth.

Any life for human beings after death would have to be a different form of life.

If God wanted people to live life only on earth, he would have to treat each one of us the same. That is, if he was to be fair or just with all of us.

In order to live a happy life on earth, we all would have to live the same length of time. Also, we would have to be free of work so we could enjoy the many wonders of the world. All people would have to be good to each other. Also, people would work together and help each other.

It is easily understood that conditions among people on earth are not like those just mentioned. Therefore, God's plan for people must extend beyond life on this earth.

What is beyond life on earth that God plans for his people?

That is a question that might seem impossible to answer. Looking at it as a human being with earthly eyes, we just can't see beyond the happenings on this earth.

It is reasonable to assume that God has a good reason for everything he has made for the future and in the past. The whole universe is the work of God.

Human beings are such a wonderful example of God's handiwork that it just is impossible to believe that they are not very important to God.

The first work that God completed in his plan for people was the creation of the earth with all that was necessary for God's people to live properly here on earth.

Next, God gave people the ability to be able to live and take care of themselves here on earth. But he also limited the number of years we can live. About 130 or 140 years, at the most, is the life span ot people on earth. That very uncertainty of the length of life here proves God has plans for people after they die.

Many hardships, sickness, and problems of all kinds face people living here. Families must be raised, one generation after another, in order to keep the human race from disappearing from the earth. God does not expect people to live under these conditions and then have them die without any kind of lasting reward for them.

God sent Christ on earth as a human being so he could tell those people who would listen to him that God loved them and had prepared a place in heaven for those who would believe in him and trust him and submit their free will to his will.

This is God's answer to his people who could not understand why they were born. This gives people a very important and definite purpose for their existence. Every event in our lives here has a purpose in preparing us for a life after death with God and other supernatural beings who are with God.

It must be understood that life on earth is a wonderful experience, with many enjoyable pleasures, and with just one condition that is absolutely necessary: we must live according to God's plan for his people.

The way people want to live as human beings can easily be very different from God's plan for them. This is the difference between a life without God after death or a supernatural life with God forever in complete happiness, without problems and suffering.

Certainly, we have to live on earth first. Then, if we are interested in serving God above everything else, with complete submission of our will to God's will, we can enjoy God's reward for every human being.

This is God's plan for his people living on earth.

III

An Analysis of
the Best Goal in Life

There are many things that interest people during their lifetime. What they will do for their life's work, is one, for example. There are hundreds of different kinds of work. Most young people put off choosing the type of work they want to do until they are through high school or college. Many others just get a job doing whatever they can.

Children seem to be attracted by firemen, policemen, doctors, nurses, teachers, etc.

The goal in life for every person should be to get the most out of living. In order to determine your goal, the true value of what you are doing must be analyzed. First, your goal must result in achieving the best for you during your life.

Believe it or not, as the years go by, your health is very important to you. In order to prove this to yourself, just take a good look around you. Go to a doctor's office and see with your own eyes how many people need medical attention.

Another good plan is to watch older people who are sixty or seventy years old. Find out from those who are sick or losing their health if they think good health is important during their lifetime. Those who just don't have good health would give all the money they possess if they could only have their health again. Many of them never will.

Look at younger people between forty and fifty years old. You will find many of them already in trouble with their health. Many have already had heart trouble and other types of sickness.

Even much younger people have health problems. Again, go to most any hospital and you will find sick people of all ages, from babies on up.

It is not hard to believe that health is a major problem to people. Of course, the young people do not think much about caring for their health. They are so busy with what they believe is a "good time' while they are young. They just keep on doing things until they are so sick they just cannot go on any more. Then they go to their doctor and usually have to go home and go to bed. It just doesn't pay to be sick and lose days or weeks of school or work in addition to the money.

So many people do this throughout their lives. They always think it won't happen again. Again, good health is very important to people of all ages.

Next, you must be building in your mind a good feeling of achievement. This means attaining a feeling of success in life. This feeling of achievement involves many accomplishments as you go through life. It is a building up of what you consider one success after another and that leads to satisfactory living.

The amazing thing is that each success or victory urges us on to a greater success. This keeps up our confidence in our ability to be successful.

It must be realized that keeping up with other people in financial success, social activities, good homes, good marriages, successful children of all ages, good jobs, etc., is very important in the minds of most people. Also, many are working very hard today so someday they can retire and do just as they please. All of these things seem to give us a feeling of importance.

It is not hard to believe we are really better and more

important than many people with whom we come in contact. If they worked as hard as we do and were as smart as us, then they might be more like us. That is what we think.

A feeling of security in life is also of great importance. Many people think that a good job is very necessary for a feeling of security. A good marriage seems to give many people a feeling of security. A good education as well good training for skilled labor will give us a feeling of security.

Certainly, money gives people a good feeling of security. It appears that if we have enough money we can have the things we want in life. The trouble is that the more money we get, the more we seem to need. One thing leads to another and we just never seem to have quite enough. If we only had more, we surely would have enough, we often think. But it goes on and on, until something finally happens that ends the upward rise in our money successes.

Feeling satisfied with our life means we are contented or completely pleased with everything. We are not disappointed or bitter about anything in our whole life. There is nothing we would want to change. We could not change the past anyway, but we could feel our lives would have been much better if certain things had not happened, maybe many years ago. So to be well satisfied with our complete life is very important to us.

Therefore, the most important goal in our life must result in the following achievements:

1. Good health
2. Feeling of success
3. Feeling of importance
4. Feeling of security
5. Feeling satisfied with life

Thus, it is very important that people seek the proper goal in life in order to keep them in the right state of mind. The best goal is the one that is truly satisfying as time goes on.

People seek to attain many different types of goals. Very often people start their way through life without much serious thinking or planning. That is the reason they get into all kinds of problems—they are not trying to do things that are best for them. Our weak and ignorant human nature gets us into all kinds of trouble. To live a satisfying life, then, people must carefully plan how they are going to live so they can make life a very satisfactory experience.

IV

The Fundamentals of Proper Character

The lives of many people are very difficult because they do not understand the basic facts involved in proper living. This involves themselves as well as other people with whom they come in contact.

Many people are doing things harmful to themselves as a result of improper training when they were children. They just don't know a better way. Therefore, in order to change to the proper way of living, they must teach themselves a new and better way of life.

Now we can consider the best way to act toward ourselves and also toward other people:

1. Sincerity in purpose—There is no use trying to deceive ourselves about anything. Many people lie about something because they do not want the other person to know the truth. Maybe the other person cannot prove you are telling a lie, but this does not change the situation with you. It is still not the truth in your own mind.

In order to develop sincerity, a person must try to do what his reasoning tells him is best in the end. It doesn't make any difference whether we like the best way or not. Our intelligence tells us to make the best decision we can in solving a problem. We just are not satisfied when we make a poor decision. Many times a person is tempted to do whatever is easy. We avoid doing the difficult; therefore, we don't solve our problem, we only make it more difficult.

To be sincere when we tell another person we will do

something is most important. If you can't do something he wants, simply tell him you just will not be able to do it. Do not disappoint him by saying yes, and then not do it. How would you like to have that happen to you?

It may take a little courage to say no, but that is the best way and it is very important in the proper training of your mind and character.

In case you just can't say no, tell the person you cannot decide yes or no at that time. Also, you can tell him you will wait and let nature take its course. The most important thing is not to deceive the other person.

2. Dependability—This involves effort on your part, but it certainly is very important in getting the most out of your life.

Again, consider how you feel when a person you are dealing with does not do what he says he will do. There is no use getting mad at him. That does not do any good. The final result is that you just cannot depend on him. So don't put your faith and trust in him. Spend your effort and time developing your own dependability.

If there is something to be done that is not important, do not promise to do it. If it is important and you have promised to do it for another person, then get it done, or else let him know in advance that you cannot do it as you had planned. You almost always satisfy the other person by telling him you can't come as planned. He knows you are sincere and want to do what you promise. Then be sure to follow through with your promise as soon as possible.

3. Honesty—This is also involved with sincerity and dependability. Many times in your life you will be tempted to be dishonest. You will know in your own mind whether you are thinking honestly about the problem you have to solve. Would you like to be treated the same as you are treating the other person? That is a very good way to help you decide.

In order for people to trust you, they must feel you have been fair and honest in your dealings with them. There is nothing that is more mind- and soul-satisfying to a person than to have other people trust him. There is no substitute for honesty. A person is either honest or dishonest. It is a shame, but a person can be honest in almost all of his dealings, then dishonest in only a few of them, and the result is that other people are confused and do not know whether to trust this person or not.

Even worse, when a person is dishonest even one time, he is disturbed and his subconscious mind is confused because he has given a "yes" and a "no" about the same thing. What will he do next time? Is it "yes" or "no"—to be honest or to be deceitful? The truth is, being honest is just like everything else we must decide; the more times we make an honest decision, the easier it is the next time.

Therefore, even if it really hurts us to be fair and honest, we are rewarded by what we can call a satisfied conscience. To be mentally tormented by our wrongdoings is very detrimental to a person.

If we have been unfair with other people, the only thing we can do is to go back to them, if we can, and straighten the matter out. Yes, even more than fair. That is what gives us a satisfied mental condition.

4. Being fair with ourselves—This is a little difficult to analyze. But we know when we feel satisfied in our own mind that we have treated ourselves fair. Remember, we do not have to submit our will to people who want to take advantage of us. We can say no in a very nice way. We do not have to be fooled by deceitful people because they are greedy and want to receive a lot more than they give the person with whom they are dealing.

The real answer in finding people who are honest and really want to render a service to their customers is to ask other people who know the business man. What is their opinion about him? Do they think he is honest and dependable? Most people will let you know in some way what they think of him. If he is honest, they will tell you right out. If they think he can't be trusted, they will let you know, perhaps without saying right out that he is dishonest.

People who are deceitful and dishonest just can't get along with the people who know them. If they are in business, they just can't stay in the same place. They have to move some other place where they are not known.

Also, people who work for others can't keep a job if they are deceitful and dishonest. They have to go from one job to another. So in being honest with ourselves, we must try to protect ourselves against other people who want to take advantage of us.

We are not obligated to strangers who just happen to come along. If they are hungry, feed them, but you do not have to take them into your home. Many people just wandering around have learned to depend on others to give them food and a place to stay. They do not care about working to support themselves. By just being respectful to them you can do them far more good than by taking care of them and then telling them they are no good and sending them away. We must remember that every person on earth belongs to God, and we must be respectful to them in our words and actions. But that is all. They have a right to live any kind of life they want; that is up to them. They still have the obligation of helping themselves as much as possible.

If a person is working for someone else, he will be honest with himself if he tries to do good work for his employer. Also, he must be dependable in getting to work. If he is a good worker, he will not have to worry about getting a job. If he loses one job or feels he must change jobs in fairness to himself, he will soon find another job. There have never been enough good workers to fill the demand. Also, there is always an oversupply of poor workers. So by being fair with yourself and honestly trying to do good work, you will help yourself more than anyone else.

By being careful and honest with other people, you will make life much easier for yourself. People will be pleased to see you, and honest people will do what they can for you.

5. Responsibility to other people—During our life we come in contact with many other people. The big question is, how shall we act toward them? What shall we do when they try to take advantage of us?

The most important fact to consider in our relationship with other people is that every person on earth belongs to God. There are just no exceptions to this because God is the creator of everything. If we have respect for God, we will have respect for his people. But because we have respect for other people, this does not mean that we have to do what they want us to do or believe as they would like to have us believe.

The only exception to this is that children, when they are small, cannot reason for themselves and must follow and imitate their parents or other people. As soon as they are old enough to think for themselves, they begin to choose by saying yes or no.

When there is some way we can help other people, we must first decide if what they want will be good for them. We must act according to the principle that we should only do things that are good for us and will actually help us, rather than just satisfy us because we think we want or need something. This same principle is to be used with other people.

Next, the question is whether or not the other person sincerely wants the help we can give him. If he does not want our help, there is nothing we can do for him. All of our efforts will be in vain. Then the only influence we can have on the other person is by our example.

How do we react when we don't have our own way? Are we frustrated, do we get mad? Because of our ignorance and the weakness in human nature, it is very human to get mad when we don't have our own way. At the very least, we are disappointed and discouraged when things do not go the way we want them.

How do we react when other people do not get mad at something they do not like? Certainly, without any question, it makes us respect them more if they do not display their anger or disappointment.

The easy way to satisfy ourselves when these things happen is to remind ourselves that the other person belongs to God. It does not make any difference how insignificant or "low-down" the other person may be, he still belongs to God. Every person, including all the social outcasts, are creatures of God.

Our conscience tells us whether we have shown respect to other people or not. If we feel satisfied with our actions, we know we have been respectful to them.

Our final responsibility to other people is that we make the best decision we can about what to do. The best we can do is all we can do. It always helps to try to think how we would like to be treated if we were in their place. When we are doing the best for ourselves, we are following the fundamentals of proper character as discussed in this chapter.

Certainly, good character is very important if we are to get the most out of life.

V

The Most Important Decision to Make in Your Life

Whether we like it or not, God is the greatest power or supernatural force in the universe. Since we are his creatures, he has absolute control of every person on earth.

It seems like people are quite free to do what they want, but even during our day-to-day living on earth, we are subject to the forces of nature.

Who controls nature? No one else but God.

No one can change the forces of nature any more than they can change God. There is absolutely no escape from the control and power of God. There is no place where God does not have complete power.

As a result, human beings have no choice but to recognize this supreme and complete power of an unknown and unseen God. That is, if they want to be honest with themselves.

Now we come to the greatest decision in the *life and eternity* of a weak and ignorant human being.

What are we going to do about God?

There are three choices we have which God has made possible for us:

1. We can try to fight what God wants.
2. We can ignore him and pretend that we don't know anything about him.
3. We can recognize his power over us and admit we are helpless and cannot win over God.

Let us first consider choice number one.

There are many times that people actually fight what God wants. It must be remembered that nature, with all of the problems that it creates for human beings, is under the direct control of God. Many times children wish they were grown up so they could be like adults. Of course, all they understand about adult life is what they can see as a child. Therefore, their ideas about being grown-up are usually not according to reality. Grown up people, on the other hand, who just can't seem to adjust to being adults, often wish they were children. But you just can't change nature according to God's plan.

Certainly parents fight to help their children. Many would do anything they could to save the life of a child. What can they do if a child dies? There is no way to bring it back to life. Some parents still can't give up the idea that God was cruel and wrong in allowing their child to die. They may be bitter towards God for a long time.

So it is impossible for people to fight against what God allows to happen. They cannot win against God or nature. But they can make themselves very miserable and make living much more difficult. People cannot be satisfied and miserable at the same time.

Even with health, people must live and eat according to nature and God's plan or else they must take the consequences. Nature tries to help our bodies for a long time. Many years may go by, but nature finally just can't keep the body healthy any longer and sickness takes over. Sometimes death results when people do not respond to the many warnings of nature. These people were mistaken in believing they could live and eat anyway they wanted.

So another fight is lost with nature and God.

What good does it do to get mad at God? There is nothing you can do about it.

Next, we can consider choice number two: Ignore God and pretend that we don't know anything about him.

What if we try to convince ourselves that God is so far away he doesn't care about us? We can't see him anyway. How do we know he is even fair with us? How does it happen that we always seem to be the ones to have hard luck so many times?

That is where our conscience still does not allow us to ignore God. Every normal person can understand that a power that is supernatural had to create everything that exists in the entire universe. It doesn't matter how it was developed or how many millions of years it took for creation. The answer is always the same: some supernatural power had to be the cause of the beginning of everything.

So people who think they can get along without the help of God are not fooling anyone but themselves. Imagine any person honestly believing he can get along without any help from our creator. It is impossible, but a person could attempt it through his free will, given to him by God. But still he must suffer the consequences when he is going against nature or God.

Let us consider choice number three: We can recognize God's power over his people and admit we are helpless and cannot win over him.

Certainly, if we want to do what is the very best for us, and get the most out of life, we will have to admit God's superiority over us. When we submit our will to God, we can have confidence and know that whatever God allows to happen will be for the best in the end.

Again we must recognize the supernatural power of God to control every person he has created. When we consider the power of God, our reasoning tells us the impossibility of a human being overcoming or stopping what God wants to happen. So people might just as well make up their minds to give in to whatever God wants. The quicker we do this, the better it is for us.

First, we can tell God in the best way we know how that we will give in to him. It is good to remember that God is not the only one we will give in to during our life. Many times in our life we must give in to other people, whether we like it or not. This is very good proof of our ability to submit our will to either God or people.

Our best choice is to put our faith and trust in God. Whom could we trust among people and have that feeling of confidence that comes with faith in God? Certainly no human being can compare with God. People might want to help, but every person is equally helpless against the supernatural power of God. All we can do is accept the help we can get from other people that is good for us, and then ask God for his help when the problem is beyond human beings.

Now is the time to realize, without any doubt, that the most important decision of our life is to put God first in everything and submit our will to him at all times. If this decision cannot be made, there is no reason to read any more of this book. The rest of the book is written to explain how and why God is all important to people in their daily lives.

VI

How God Treats His People

It is a shame that so many people have such a cloudy and mistaken idea about God our creator.

The unending power and stability of God can be seen all around us in many different ways, such as the sun that heats the world with the proper degree of heat and the other elements necessary for us to have food and keep us alive. God is constantly providing, through nature, everything necessary to make the earth's conditions suitable for people to live in. So we must giae God credit for giving his people the earth to live on and for taking care of it for them.

How does it happen that so many people have a great fear of God? They just wonder what he is going to do next to hurt them. One thing that is part of our human nature is to fear the unknown.

Even in our day-to-day problems, we are almost always afraid of anything that is new and unknown to us. Work that we have not done before and have no previous knowledge about puts a fear into us that makes us believe we can't do it. Usually it is with the help of another person who has learned how to do this work that we learn.

If a person wants to learn to drive a car, he just can't get back of the steering wheel and drive off without any knowledge of what to do.

Why can't he just get the car out on the road and go places like other people who can drive a car?

Some people imagine they can do this, but anyone who stops to think, will understand that he just does not know how to drive a car. This understanding is what puts the fear in his mind. He has been honest with himself and knows he'd better have help and learn to drive a car first. Then he can drive like other people who already have been trained to drive.

We might call this attempt to do something without training or knowledge an "impulsive attempt," without any basic reasoning or previous knowledge. The result usually is that we get in serious trouble and we suddenly panic through fear, just because we didn't know what we were trying to accomplish.

These things are just minor events in our life, but they demonstrate the fact that fear of the unknown causes panic and confusion in our mind. It follows, then, that weak and ignorant human beings are normal in their fears of the unknown.

Since God is the greatest unknown and supernatural force in our lives, it is very natural for us to wonder what he is like.

How can we analyze what God might be like?

It is very easy for people to compare God with human beings, without even realizing what they are doing. Our reasoning power tells us that in most ways human beings are completely insignificant in comparison with God in their ability to do things. People just cannot create anything and put life into it. Even if they could, it would only be through the help of God.

Since God created human beings, we know he created them just exactly as he wanted them to be. Even if God did make mistakes, and we know he is perfection in comparison to human beings in his ability to do things, God would never make billions of mistakes in creating people. So the truth is that people are just exactly the way God wanted them to be.

Basic human nature and our physical bodies are all in accordance to God's plan. The biggest difference is that no two people are exactly the same in size, appearance, abilities, or mental makeup. Even if no two people are alike, it doesn't make any difference, because people must depend on God. God does not depend on people. He has no need for it. Also, God does not need any help from people in his tremendous work of creation.

It doesn't make any difference what man does; he needs the work and help of God first. God always comes first. Even if man acts in direct opposition to God's will, God must allow man to act as he does.

1. *Does God actually harm people?*

Without understanding what God's true motive is, it can easily appear to a human being that God is actually harming people, maybe even killing them, directly or indirectly.

2. *Maybe God just does not care what happens to his people?*

Many times it certainly appears that God does not care what happens to his people: there are so many problems in life, so many sick people, both physically and mentally; there is so much uncertainty about everything we might try to do; the troubles that people cause for each other are many; there are so many failures in what we try to do day by day.

Where is God while all these things are happening to his people?

Where God is, no person knows, but we do know that God is not attempting to control what people do or how they use their intelligence. God even lets whole nations of people fight wars with each other, perhaps with one nation destroying another or at least taking them over and subjecting them to the utmost cruelty and torture. It certainly reminds us of the terrible torture and death they imposed on Christ, the son of God.

Still, God made no effort to stop it.

Christ himself even said, "Forgive them Father because they know not what they are doing." At the same time, Christ was dying a terrible death on the cross.

These are just a few of the reasons why people have a hard time trying to understand how God acts toward his creatures.

Suppose we want to believe that God does respect his people?

1. God provides plenty of food for his people, first through the creation of fruits, vegetables, and everything else needed. All God demands from his people is that they must prepare the soil and do the rest of the work necessary for them to grow food to live on.

2. God provides his people with good bodies and the mental capacity to help them get through life on earth.

3. God creates his people so they can enjoy living. Much pleasure and satisfaction can be enjoyed by parents in raising a family. A family can be the most enjoyable way of life with other people. Of course, they must live in accordance with the way God wants them to. They just can't live any way they want to. There must be a program of cooperation, fairness, and understanding among the members of the family. Otherwise, there will be trouble between brothers and sisters, fathers and mothers.

God has made it possible for members of a family to work together and be happy. But they must all be working for one goal in life, that is, to follow God and Christ the best way they can. All work together and each one learns to put his faith and trust in God and Christ instead of other people or material possessions.

4. Even if people try to get along together and work hard to be successful, there are still numerous events in their lives that make life very uncertain.

5. Quite a few people are trying to tell us that God is

waiting some place, watching his people, just waiting for them to make one or more mistakes. These mistakes are called sins against God our creator. Also, we are told by these people that God has prepared terrible punishment for evil people who have sinned against him.

Many people believe the story of the eating of forbidden fruit by our first parents. God is supposed to have changed the conditions of the whole world and all the people living here because of his anger at the disobedience of the first parents on earth.

All people are supposed to share the guilt and suffer the same as the first parents. Because of this eating of the apple, the lives of all future people were supposed to have been changed by God. First, he drove them out of Paradise. This was a place where people could live forever without any problems. They would have enjoyed complete happiness. There was to be no work, no sickness, and life would last forever. God must have changed his mind about the way people have to live on earth after the first parents ate the forbidden apples.

It is necessary to disagree with this story about God and the first man and woman he created.

What does our reasoning power tell us?

If God created the earth and set up the whole program for his people on earth, and we know this took millions of years, at least, why should one act of disobedience make God change his mind about everything he had planned for people?

It doesn't take much arithmetic to figure out the fact that if no person ever died, sometime later the number of people on earth at one time would be enough to cover the entire land. Think how fast the number of people would multiply through reproduction—every new generation would bring five or six times as many people as the generation before. This could happen every fifteen or twenty years at the most.

Another reason for disagreement is the fact that God sent

Christ on earth to tell people that God wanted them to be able to live in heaven with him. How can people get to heaven without leaving this earth? How can we, as human beings, be in two places at the same time.

It is common knowledge that people have no choice but to stay here on earth while they are alive. Gravity around the earth keeps us here. We can't even fall off the earth.

The reason Christ came to earth was to tell the people the truth about God waiting in heaven for his people to die, so they could come to heaven and be with him.

The only condition that God required of his people was that they absolutely must submit their will to his will. This also meant that people must trust God and try to follow his plan for them on earth until they died a physical death.

So now we get back to God and his method of dealing with his people.

Without any doubt, we certainly can believe what we see and know about living things on earth. All of God's creatures live and die sooner or later.

Now the big question is, how does God actually treat his people when we know the truth about how people have to live on earth?

How can we trust God when we know so little about him?

Our reason tells us there are some people we know that we can trust to quite a degree. Why do we trust them? Just because they have never lied to us, they have never tried to hurt us, in fact, they have the knowledge and the respect to help us when we are in need of help. That is the reason we feel we can trust them.

If we can trust some people, why can't we trust God our creator?

Can we trust our doctor and even put our life in his hands, and then, at the same time, be afraid of God and fear to trust him?

Reasoning again tells us of the supernatural power of God our creator.

We should place our trust and faith in God to the greatest extent of our ability as human beings. We can decide that God is the greatest power and has the supernatural ability to help his people in any way they might need help. At first, it will be a blind faith in God to turn ourselves over to him and be completely dependent on him.

If a small child did not give himself completely over to the help and care of his mother or father, how could he get along? He just could not live without their help or the help of other people.

In considering people giving themselves up to God, we can reason that people just cannot live the way God has made it possible unless they turn their lives over to him. We must accept our lives the way God has allowed them to be. We must take what comes, after we have done the best we can.

Sometimes it takes a long time to understand that God is doing the very best for us. As the years go by, we can look back and better understand that under his supervision, nothing but the very best from God himself ever happens to us in our life.

God is controlling our life for us just the same as parents should help and guide their children. The big difference between God and parents is the infallability of God in helping us. God never makes any mistakes, but even the best parents are still human beings and are subject to human errors.

VII

Trying to Live
Your Own Life

Freedom of choice is one of the greatest gifts God has given his people. Yet there are not very many who feel they are free to do as they please.

There is something in the minds of people that seems to drive them on to do what they really want. This is true even in small children. They want to have their way about things. It isn't very long before they learn to say yes or no.

Certainly, by the time children reach their teenage years, they are seeking to act for themselves. They are trying to establish themselves as individuals, each one trying to live his own life. This is in accordance with God's plan for his people. We find young people trying to make the change from babyhood to adulthood. Of course, this period takes a number of years, maybe eighteen or twenty.

But we must remember that the change is from the complete dependence of a baby to a nearly complete independence as an adult. Of course, the independence the person has achieved as an adult depends on his training as a child by his parents and also on what this person has done to develop his own independence.

By independent people, we mean people that are fairly well able to take care of themselves in day-to-day living. This means independent living as far as other people are concerned.

Because we are weak and ignorant creatures belonging to God, our dependence on God never changes, even from before the time we are born. How long we have to depend on God, no human being will ever know, but certainly as long as we live on earth.

Thus we find people old enough to be considered adults. We certainly can understand they have been given by God himself the ability to choose whether they want to do a thing or not. This ability was given them before they were old enough to be teenagers. And still you are going to find that most teenagers feel that they just cannot have their own way about many things. If God has given them the ability to choose for themselves, through free will, and still they can't do as they please, there is something wrong.

This is a very serious and important fact about their lives. They still want to live their lives the way *they want.* They certainly resent having other people tell them what to do.

It is well to remember that every person of normal intelligence, regardless of age, feels the same way as teenagers. We all want to have our own way at least about certain things.

By the time people reach adulthood, they find themselves involved with all the problems that come with being an adult. The training they received from parents or others, and the results of their own acts, are beginning to stand out. These things are beginning to bear fruit in their life. Life just isn't a bed of roses. It certainly is not as it appeared to be when they were small chlidren.

If only children would be trained by their parents to go to God and Christ when they were faced with problems. This would make life a most wonderful experience as they lived year by year, until God took them to be with him in heaven. But too many parents are not able to seek the help of God themselves, so we cannot expect parents to teach their children what they can't do for themselves. The next best thing is for each person who is old enough to find out he needs help and to reason it out for himself.

First, it is necessary to admit to himself that he just cannot do many things he would like to do. It doesn't make any difference how hard he might try.

Second, he must realize that all other people are in the same position as he is in. They can't do the things for him that he might need help with. Also, they can't solve many of their own problems.

Third, he must understand that there are no parents on earth who are able to help their children with all the problems that might come along. Also, there are no parents on earth who can train their children as they might be trained. Every parent has his weakness, just the same as every child.

Most of us fall in this category. So the answer just has to be that human beings can't help themselves or other people in solving many important problems in their life on earth. So the only thing left to do is to seek the help of the supernatural. That can only mean God.

Why should we think God can help us?

Certainly, if God has the power to create people, he must have the power to help his creatures.

As human beings, we can never even begin to know what God is like. But we don't have to know all these things. What we want to know is whether God is able to help us when we need his help.

First, let us be sure no one else can help us. Next, be sure we cannot help ourselves. After we have tried every way known to us to get help, what is there left for us to do? If the problem is very important and we can't get an answer, what do we do next? Maybe we can forget it? Very good, if we can, but what about the problems you can't forget and cannot get an answer for?

You probably not only have a problem, but a conflict in

your mind. So you go along now with an extra mental burden you didn't have before.

There is no other place to go for help—only God himself. Maybe you think God is mad at you. Maybe you think he is so far away he doesn't know about you and your problem. Maybe you are afraid of God and hope he doesn't know all the so-called sins you have committed. But still, there is no place else to go for help, only God.

So finally, you remember you are going to do the best you can to get the most out of your life. Your reasoning tells you that God is your last resort for help. Still, maybe God won't help you, and you hesitate. Maybe you are too proud to ask God for help. At last, you just give up and hope you will get through this problem all right. Maybe a friend tells you to just forget it.

Time goes on and for some reason or other this same problem comes into your life again. Only this time, it is worse than the last time. Other problems seem to come along with it.

And you find you just don't seem to be able to have your own way about things in your life. Just about the time it looks like everything is coming your way, something turns up to spoil it for you. It just seems that life is one problem after another.

Life with all its problems and uncertainties, just keeps going its course. It almost seems that life is like a ride down a very swift and treacherous river in a boat. Maybe you can guide the boat to some extent and maybe you cannot. Along the way you can see many other boats that have already been smashed on the rocks and the people have already lost their lives. All you can do is to keep on going the best way you can.

Wouldn't it be wonderful if you only had some supernatural power that you could always depend on for help if you got in trouble? The only drawback is that you would have to submit your will to this supernatural force and take whatever happened.

What if you could learn by experience, through the years, that it didn't make any difference what happened, as long as you trusted this unseen supernatural power and everything turned out for the best for you? After all, remember, you have no other choice anyway, in spite of your freedom.

Many important events in your life concern things no one has any choice about. A person certainly has no choice about when he is born into this world. Neither does he have any choice of parents. As a child, he must accept the kind of training he gets.

Usually a person has no choice about sickness and death. People just cannot stop the force of nature that might take their life and destroy their homes. There are many other examples of events a person cannot control during his life.

So, in spite of the free will God has given his people, important happenings in a lifetime cannot be controlled by human beings.

VIII

Reason Proves God Is Our Best Help

It is not hard to decide through reason that often, in a lifetime, people face problems they cannot take care of themselves.

We can go right back to the truth that God has created his people in a way that they must depend on him, whether they want to or not. This is the result of God's power to create and control everything he has created. Since God is the highest form of supernatural power, he is the most logical source of help for people on earth.

Still, it is difficult for people to put their faith and trust in an unknown God. If we could only see him and talk to him it would help quite a bit. But God has created people with the ability to understand that he exists somewhere, unknown to them.

Anything people attempt to accomplish requires help of some kind. Maybe they can read out of a book and learn how to do what they are planning. Maybe they have to learn by trying to do it. This might require a lot of time and effort. It would take a trial and error method. Thus, they could make numerous mistakes before they learned.

People can also learn a great deal by having other people help them.

If there were no colleges and universities with teachers and books to learn from, how many doctors or lawyers or other professional people would we have in the world today?

47

By the same reasoning, how can we learn to seek the help of God?

It is only by *trying* to learn that we can make progress in anything we want to accomplish. Just think of all the studying and effort it takes for a person to become a doctor. Many years of hard work must be completed to achieve the ability to practice medicine. I suppose even state tests must be passed before a doctor can open his office. Also, an internship must be completed.

So it is with God. A person just can't learn to seek his help without effort.

How long would it take a person to be able to become a doctor if he spent one hour per week learning? Never in his lifetime would he get through with his training. The same holds true with most any other work people might try to learn.

If parents spent one hour per week in raising their children, how far would they get?

Even if God is our best source of help, people must first decide they need his help. Next, they must decide to turn their minds to him and tell him they realize they need his help. Then they must ask God for help the best way they can.

Seeking the help of God is very much like a child seeking the help of its mother. A child is certainly sincere when it seeks the comfort and help of its mother.

Anything people can do to help themselves is good. Also, anything other people can help them with is good. The real test is the help that is needed by people when they cannot do it for themselves, or no other person can help them.

What do you do when the information in books or the way you are taught something is wrong, or you are told one thing by some people and exactly the opposite by others?

Certainly, you have a mental conflict. If it is something unimportant just forget it, or make your own decision about it. It should not make much difference one way or another.

Until a person can do otherwise, all he can do is to pray to God for help the best way he knows how. Maybe this person can decide to trust in God just a little bit. He knows through experience he can trust a good friend. God should certainly be trusted as much as a good friend.

Again, reason tells us that God has the power to help people if he wants to. Just make up your mind to give God a chance to help you. There is absolutely nothing to be lost by trusting him, especially if we don't seem to be able to get help any place else.

You just cannot get anything valuable out of life if you don't put forth the necessary effort. It is a matter of trying to get God's help day after day. Just keep on trying again and again. Faith in getting God's help will get stronger as time goes on.

Our greatest trouble with God is that we do not understand him. We must learn to understand him.

You can almost consider God as you would a good friend. That is not being fair to God, but it is a slight comparison, at least. You already know how you feel about a person who honestly tries to be a good friend.

First, you understand that this person has respect for you. This becomes apparent by the way he acts toward you. He certainly is not making fun of you, nor is he being sarcastic with you.

Second, you know that he is dependable. He demonstrates this by doing what he says he will do. He will come to visit you when he says he will.

Third, this friend will not try to deceive you. He will not

pretend he will do something by saying yes, and then not do it when the time comes.

Fourth, he will try to show his friendship by doing little things to be helpful.

Fifth, this friend will not impose on you by asking you to do things for him that you cannot do, or things that he should do for himself.

Sixth, a good friend will not keep asking for your help and never be around when you need help.

To add it all up, you know after a while whether you have a good friend or not. If he proves to be a good friend, you certainly can understand he is valuable to you.

Certainly God is the infallible friend of his people. There is absolutely nothing that ever happens to a person on earth that God cannot help him with. Any time you ask God for help you will get help some way or other. It is absolutely necessary for you to be sincere in asking God for help. You must submit your will to him. You must trust that he will do what is best for you.

Put your trust and faith in God just as you would in the best human friend you could ever find during your lifetime. Then let God take care of your problem. Leave it up to him, and you are ready to take whatever happens.

You already depend on God to do what is best for you. God knows when you trust him. God will give you strength and courage to carry you through your trouble, or else he will eliminate your problem; God always knows which is best for you.

God is absolutely worthy of your trust in him.

It does not make any difference what human being tells you that God is mad at you; there is no logical reason why God should be mad at any of his people.

It is well to note here that any person who is a good

friend of yours will not be mad at you. You may irritate him by your actions, but he will not remain angry.

However, you cannot expect to have a good friend unless you are fair with him and try to be a friend of his. Friendship just cannot be one-sided. To have a good friend, you must be a good friend.

Certainly, being a good friend and having a good friend applies to God, our "infallible friend."

IX

Proof That God Has Provided the Supernatural Help We Need

Nearly two thousand years ago God provided the supernatural help which the human race needed so badly.

During all that time prior to the coming of Christ, the people just had to live and get along the bet way they could by serving or understanding their unknown supernatural creator we call God.

It must have been the proper time for God to provide the help needed by his people, because God created us and he knows what is best for us; he knows when to provide help that is needed.

For many years, people had been expecting a redeemer to be sent by God. Prophets had foretold the coming of a redeemer.

John the Baptist preceded Christ in his public appearances and, in a way, prepared his listeners for Christ.

There were many messianic preachers both before and after John, but their methods were different from John's. All without exception declared that the sons of Abraham were the first people of the earth, and to assure a real political supremacy for them, they all had recourse to arms. Many actually claimed to be kings; others claimed they could perform miracles. A few took over other people's property and risked other's lives, though rarely their own. It never occurred to any one of them to improve their followers morally.

John went the exact opposite direction; he promised no kingdoms or supremacy; he neither touched weapons himself nor appealed to any armed force; he ignored political matters; he worked no miracles; he was poor and wore goat skins.

One moral admonition contained all his preaching: The kingdom of God is imminent; hence, change your way of thinking!

The very first word of his proclamation was "Repent"—change your way of thinking. In Hebrew the word was *shub,* which means to "return from a false road in order to set out on the right one." In both Greek and Hebrew, the concept is the same—a complete transformation in the mind of man.

A deep sincere feeling naturally seeks expression of some sort and an external physical act may be evidence and proof of an inner spiritual one. So John required those "changing their way of thinking" to confess their sins as an external manisfestation of the change, and to undergo a physical absolution as its proof and symbol.

Judaism practiced both rites on various occasions. On the Day of Atonement (Yom Kippur) the high priest performed them together, for he acknowledged the sins of the whole people and performed a special ablution on himself.

The originality of John lay in the fact that he required these rites as preparation for the kingdom of God. So what John the Baptist actually told his followers was, in plain words, as follows:

Repent—this means just change your way of thinking. (In Hebrew—change your mind).

Confess your sins—John the Baptist meant this as an external manifestation of changing their way of thinking.

Baptism in water—performing a physical ablution as proof and symbol that they had changed their way of thinking.

These rituals were required by John for the people to prove they were truly sincere in changing their minds in preparing themselves for a kingdom which concerned the spirit above all else. John the Baptist was preparing his followers for Christ, the Messiah, who was to follow John and preach the Kingdom of God, which was in heaven.

All other prophets, except ancient Israel's authentic prophets, thought the Messiah, when he came, would establish a Kingdom on earth to rule people as an earthly King. Israel's prophets insisted on works of justice rather than ceremonies of the liturgy.

John rose up as the last and final prophet. Later Jesus said, "Until John came, there were the Law and the Prophets; since then the Kingdom of God is being preached."

This certainly has to be a spiritual Kingdom of God in heaven. This means that people must seek the Kingdom of God in a spiritual kingdom instead of any kingdom on earth. It means people must try to live according to God, not according to the way people live on earth for earthly possessions and earthly achievements.

So it was John the Baptist who prepared his followers for the public appearances of Christ.

It is well to remember at this time that the purpose of Baptism, as is generally believed, is for the remission of sins, particularly the so-called "Original Sin." The Baptism in water by John the Baptist is well remembered.

It is mentioned several times that John the Baptist was very understanding, forgiving, and gentle with all people he came in contact with.

John had never seen Jesus so he did not know him. When Jesus came to the place where John was baptizing people, Jesus was apparently a penitent, but he confessed no sin. John recognized Christ, the Messiah, at that meeting. Now John could preach the fact that Christ was on his earthly mission. The Messiah was now on earth, teaching people to repent or change their minds and believe in the spiritual kingdom of God in heaven. (This information can be found in the book,

The Life of Christ by Giuseppe Ricciotti, Chapter XV, pages 267-172, The Bruce Publishing Co., Milwaukee, Wisconsin, 1947.)

There are so many historical facts that prove the existence of Christ on earth, that many things that happened during his life need not be included in these pages.

The birth of Christ came at a time when there was general peace among the nations of the world.

At different times during his life, Christ mentioned to his followers: "My peace I bring to you, my peace I give to you." He wanted the people to understand that everything he wanted to give was valuable to them.

John the Baptist prepared the way for the public appearances of Christ. So John, in reality, was telling the people that they must change their minds and change their way of living. Almost all the prophets before John had foretold that the Messiah would come in earthly power and glory, so naturally, people were looking for that kind of a person.

But John was a very simple person with no earthly ambitions or attachments, and he had been forewarned through a spiritual means that Christ was being put on earth to teach people the truth about God and his kingdom in Heaven.

Therefore, the Baptism of John could mean only one thing. It had to mean that people who would change their minds, change their way of living, and seek the spiritual kingdom of God instead of earthly things, would go out to the river Jordan and publicly admit and state these things and be baptized by John the Baptist.

The words used were "Repentance" and "Forgiveness of Sins." These were explained on previous pages.

The Public Ministry of Christ

During the first period of his teaching in Galilee, Christ continued the teaching of John the Baptist, who preached that the kingdom of God was at hand. But Christ did not speak of the founder of the kingdom of God in heaven at first.

Later, when he had gathered together a small nucleus of followers, Christ told them confidentially that he was the Messiah. They already understood, to a certain degree, that Christ's kingdom was not political and that its founder was a spiritual king.

Because of his miracles, Christ could not let people think that he was a Messiah from heaven who had come to earth to take over the world and rule it the same as an earthly king. If that were so, they would rise up in crowds to see him made king of the people. They were already being oppressed by the Roman rulers, and they wanted to get out from under that burden.

Even before the appearance of Christ with John the Baptist, the Scribes and Pharisees felt John's words sounded revolutionary to them. So they were waiting to watch Jesus and find out what he had to talk about.

Let's consider the most important acts of Jesus during his public ministry.

The first miracle performed by Jesus was the changing of the water into wine at the wedding feast in Cana.

A few months passed since Jesus had met John the Baptist in the river Jordan. The Pasch of the new year was approaching. So Jesus went to the temple in Jerusalem. There he found the outer court was in a mess with the trading of animals and the cries of the traders. Jesus made a whip of cords and drove the money changers out of the court.

Certain important Jews questioned Jesus about this, and he told them: "Destroy this temple and in three days I will raise it up."

Of course, they thought Jesus meant the building containing the temple. How could Jesus do this when it took forty-six years to build it?

The Jews wanted to know what authority Jesus had to come to the temple and do what he did.

Jesus told the Jews indirectly about his future crucifixion and then his resurrection back to life in three days. But they did not understand what he meant by these words. Let us read the words of Christ again: "Destroy this temple and in three days I will raise it up again."

The Jews had asked for a sign (or a miracle) from Jesus to prove he had divine authority, but Jesus wanted them to believe in the kingdom of God through faith, not through a miracle they could witness with their eyes.

At that time there was an outstanding Pharisee and teacher of the law named Nicodemus. He was an honest and upright man. But he was a member of the Sanhedrin, so his social position required him to be very cautious about what he did in public.

When Nicodemus saw the miracles performed by Jesus, he was deeply impressed. He was probably one of the few Pharisees who had been baptized by John the Baptist. But the training of Nicodemus warned him to be cautious about accepting Jesus, the unknown wonder worker.

So Nicodemus had a long conversation with Jesus at night in private. Nicodemus said to Jesus: "Rabbi, we know you have come as a teacher from God, for no one can work these signs that you can work unless God is with him." This man recognized that Jesus' mission was not a human mission, but something that was divine.

Jesus answered Nicodemus this way: "Amen, Amen, I say unto you, unless a man be born again, he cannot see the kingdom of God."

Nicodemus could not grasp the precise spiritual significance of these words, but to get an answer from Jesus, he pretended to be very dense and asked Jesus: "How can a man be born when he is old? Can he perhaps enter a second time into his mother's womb?"

In spite of his shrewdness, Nicodemus was put in the position of an unlearned apprentice. A person cannot see the kingdom of heaven unless he has already entered into it, and his entrance is not accomplished by human means.

So Jesus answered Nicodemus: "Amen, Amen, I say to you unless a man be born again of water (Baptism) and the Spirit, he cannot enter into the Kingdom of God. That which is born of the flesh, is flesh; and that which is born of the Spirit, is Spirit."

The new life which Jesus spoke of is bestowed by the Holy Spirit and by water and is not the effect of John's rite, a Baptism of water only and a mere symbol; it is the effect of the rite which is the fulfillment of that symbol, administered with water and the Holy Spirit. The Holy Spirit is the Baptism of Jesus.

Nicodemus said to Jesus: "How can all these things be true?"

Jesus replied: "You are a teacher in Israel and do not know these things? What do you teach, if you do not teach the action of the Spirit on the soul?"

Despite his talk with Jesus, Nicodemus did not become a true disciple of Jesus, yet he was always kindly disposed toward him. He dared to speak a kind word for Jesus in the Sanhedrin. Also, he spent a considerable amount of money for spices to prepare Jesus' body for burial after the crucifixion.

After Nicodemus' visit, Jesus remained in Judea for some time. Here he had more freedom of action away from the suspicious vigilance of the ancients and the Pharisees.

One day the disciples of John the Baptist were arguing with a certain Jew about purification. John the Baptist replied in a very joyous voice: "No one can receive anything unless it is given him from heaven. You yourselves bear witness that I said: I am not the Christ (Messiah), but have been sent before him. This is my joy fulfilled. Christ must increase but I must decrease." This was John's last testimony. Finally, John was put in prison.

There were many miracles performed by Jesus: he saved the life of a child of an official of the royal court at Capernaum; he healed the mother-in-law of Peter, who was old and had "great fever"; he cured a leper of his terrible illness.

After this news had spread among the Scribes and the Pharisees, they began to watch Jesus as they had John the Baptist. So Jesus went to the desert and prayed.

Later, Jesus came back and preached again in public, while the Pharisees and doctors of the law had not, as yet, formed a judgment of Jesus, the new prophet.

The Scribes and the Pharisees were highly offended when Jesus attended a banquet given for him and his disciples by a tax collector. How could Jesus lower himself to eat and drink with the publicans and sinners?

Jesus answered them: "I have come to call sinners, not the just. I desire mercy and not sacrifice."

So Jesus was beginning to let the Pharisees know that he was not preaching the old traditions of the Jews.

Then Jesus did not insist on "fasting," although it had assumed supreme importance among the Pharisees. Also, the Pharisees condemned Jesus for not keeping the Sabbath. The old law did not permit work to be done on the Sabbath. Jesus told them: "The Sabbath was made for man and not man for the Sabbath. Therefore the Son of Man is Lord even of the Sabbath."

But the Pharisees were too proud of their Sabbath to let Jesus be Lord of that too. So the high priests and the Pharisees provided the vicious and jealous opposition to Jesus that finally led to his crucifixion.

In the meantime, Jesus had his ministry to complete, so

he kept on journeying through villages and towns, preaching and proclaiming the good tidings of the kingdom of God. His twelve disciples followed him while he was preaching his mission on earth and confirming his preaching with miracles.

The crowds thronged to Jesus, attracted not only by the effectiveness of his teachings, but even more by the immediate benefits of his miracles.

After Jesus had performed the miracle of the Bread and the Fish, to feed over 5,000 people who had gathered to listen to him, he later delivered the discourse on the "Bread of Life."

Some of those who had eaten of the bread and fish asked Jesus: "Rabbi, when did you come here?"

Jesus answered: "Amen, Amen, I say unto you, you seek me, not because you have seen signs, but because you have eaten the loaves and have been filled."

The signs of which Jesus spoke were the miracles he had performed in proof of his mission. They were thinking of the material benefit to be derived from the miracles he performed.

So Jesus told them: "Do not labor for the food that perishes, but for that which endures unto life everlasting, which the Son of Man will give you. For upon him the Father, God himself has set his seal." Jesus had received his authority not from men but from God in heaven.

His followers then asked Jesus: "What are we to do in order to perform the works of God?" They were referring to the words Jesus had told them: "Labor for the food that endures unto life everlasting."

Jesus then answered: "This is the work of God that you believe in him whom God has sent."

This means that people should believe in Jesus, even when his word disappoints their hopes and dispels their dreams; they should believe in his kingdom, even if it is a complete denial of their way of thinking.

But his listeners were not satisfied; they wanted to know

what Jesus would do so they could see and believe him. They said: "Our fathers ate the manna in the desert, as it is written: Bread from heaven he gave them to eat. What work do you perform?"

Two things were directly implied during this discussion: the work of Moses with its "sign" or seal, the manna from heaven; and the work of Jesus, with its most recent sign, the multiplication of the loaves and fish of Bethsaida. The other miracles performed by Jesus were not even considered by these people. The question was a reproach to Jesus and placed him second to Moses.

If Jesus wanted people to have faith in his invisible and intangible "kingdom," then let him work "signs" at least equal to those of Moses.

This discussion brought them to a point where a choice had to be made between Jesus and Moses: Moses and his work on the one hand, and Jesus and his "kingdom" on the other. Which of these two was the greater?

Jesus tells them directly and without leaving any doubt in their minds: "Amen, Amen, I say unto you Moses did not give you the bread from heaven. For the bread of heaven is that which comes down from heaven and gives life to the world."

The judgment of those challenging Jesus was changed. Jesus was greater than Moses since heaven was greater than earth. Jesus, not Moses, came down from heaven and gave life to the world. It was he who was truly "the bread from heaven."

But they still had their minds on material things, and one explained: "Lord give us this bread always."

Again Jesus answered: "I am the bread of life. He who comes to me shall not hunger, and he who believes in me shall never thirst. But I have told you and you have seen me and you do not believe."

There must have been a great deal of discussion in the city about these statements made by Jesus, and people must have wanted to hear more.

At his next meeting in the synagogue, the Jews were talking against him because they rejected his teaching because he had told them: "I am the bread that has come down from heaven." They kept saying: "Is this not Jesus, the son of Joseph, whose father and mother we know? How then can he say 'I have come down from heaven'?"

Again Jesus came back to the question of the bread and told them: "I am the bread of life. Your fathers ate the manna in the desert, and have died. But this is the bread that comes down from heaven so that if anyone eat of it, he will not die. I am the living bread that has come down from heaven. If anyone eat of this bread he shall live forever; and the bread I will give is my flesh for the life of the world."

At this point the unfriendly Jews had much more reason to be dumbfounded. Before, Jesus had said: "to be born again of the spirit and of water springing up into life everlasting."

These statements could be taken figuratively, just as the phrase "bread of life." This phrase also could be taken the same way as when Christ first mentioned it and applied it to himself.

Jesus came back to the very same expression, and as if to avoid any possible symbolic misunderstanding, he declared that this bread was "his flesh" given for the life of the world. When Jesus spoke of his flesh as "bread" he was not using a symbol.

His audience in the synagogue at Capernaum understood Jesus perfectly. They began to argue with each other: "How can this man give us his flesh to eat?"

This was a very solemn and decisive moment. It was now up to Jesus to define his meaning and make it absolutely clear whether his words were to be taken as a metaphor or as a plain, absolute statement of fact.

Jesus again answered to make it absolutely clear to them: "Amen, Amen, I say unto you, unless you eat the flesh of the Son of man, and drink his blood, you shall not have life in you. He who eats my flesh and drinks my blood has life everlasting and I will raise him up on the last day. For my flesh is food indeed and my blood is drink indeed. He who eats my flesh and drinks my blood abides in me and I in him. As the living Father has sent me; and as I live because of the Father, so he who eats me, he shall live because of me. This is the bread that has come down from heaven. It shall not be as it was with your fathers who ate the manna and died. He who eats this bread shall live forever."

After these words, the audience of Jesus had no further doubts about what he meant. They could not have been more clear or more precise. Jesus had plainly repeated that his flesh was true food and his blood true drink, and that to have eternal life it was necessary to eat of that flesh and drink of that blood.

Many of the disciples of Jesus were scandalized by these words. They could not listen to them without a feeling of revulsion. Evidently, their thoughts were literal and suggested something of a cannibal nature.

Jesus, knowing his disciples were murmuring against him, said: "Does this scandalize you? What then if you should see the Son of man ascending where he was before? It is the spirit that gives life; the flesh profits nothing; the words I have spoken to you are spirit and life."

Jesus considered this last sentence to be sufficient to dispel the literal fear of some form of cannibalism. But these words retained their full literal significance.

The indispensable thing was to have faith in him, and the last confirmation of this faith would be to see the Son of man ascending into heaven, whence he had descended as the living bread—heavenly bread, heavenly flesh.

From this time on, many of the followers of Jesus turned away and left him. But the twelve apostles remained faithful. One day, Jesus said to them: "Do you also wish to go away?"

Simon Peter answered him: "Lord, to whom shall we go? You have the words of eternal life, and we have come to believe and to know that you are the Holy One of God."

John did not return to this subject, and the promise of the Bread of Life is not mentioned again by John. John omits the institution of the Holy Eucharist because it had already been narrated by all three Synoptists, and his listeners were well acquainted with it. John records this promise of the "Holy Eucharist" because the Synoptists had omitted it.

There is much more written about the life of Jesus but it is not necessary to go into here. The main point to remember is that the enmity of the Scribes and the Pharisees toward Christ kept increasing because of Christ's preaching and his miracles. Also, Jesus did not let the old laws stop him from performing miracles on the Sabbath.

The Pharisees and Scribes tried to humiliate Jesus personally and discredit him among the people. They noticed that his disciples did not wash their hands before eating. This was a serious violation of "the tradition of the ancients." It was a terrible misdemeanor equivalent (according to rabbinical opinion) to "frequenting a harlot," and the penalty for it was being uprooted from the world.

As soon as the official critics discovered this "crime," they denounced it to Jesus as he was responsible for his disciples.

Jesus accepted the challenge, but he rose from this particular consideration to much more general ones.

All this washing of hands and dishes has been prescribed by the "tradition of the ancients" very well. But the "ancients" are not God, and their tradition is not the law of God, which is infinitely greater. Hence, it is necessary to follow the law of God.

The law of God prescribed that men honor their fathers and mothers and help them materially when this was necessary. The Rabbis, on the other hand, established the rule that if an Israelite decided to offer a certain object to the temple, that offering could go nowhere but into the temple treasury. In such instances, it was sufficient to pronounce the word *Corban* (sacred offering), and the object so designated became holy temple property.

It often happened, therefore, that an ill-disposed son would declare all his possessions *Corban,* and no one, not even his father and mother, though they might be dying of hunger, could touch anything belonging to this son.

The son, however, could continue to enjoy the goods he had so consecrated until he had actually consigned them to the temple, or else he managed to find some means of avoiding their donation to the treasury. This applied also to the Rabbi, and there were many loopholes in the law.

Since this was the law, Jesus answered his hecklers: "How nicely you set aside the commandment of God in order to save your tradition."

Moses said: "Honor your father and mother; and he who curses father or mother, let him surely die. But you say, if a man says to his father or mother, whatever support you might have had from me is now *Corban;* and so you no longer allow him to do anything for his father or mother thus annulling the word of God by means of your *tradition* which you have handed down."

And Jesus said: "Many other things similar you are doing."

The conclusion is based on a passage in Isaias. Jesus said: "Hypocrites! Well did Isaias prophesy of you saying; this people honors me with their lips, but their heart is far from me;

but in vain do they worship me, teaching the precepts of men."

After about a year and a half of traveling and teaching, Jesus decided it was time to tell the apostles that he was truly the Son of God. Suddenly, Jesus asked his disciples: "Who do men say I am?" They answered that some thought he was Elias, some said John the Baptist, others thought he might be an ancient prophet come to life again.

And Jesus then said: "And whom do you say that I am?"

Simon Peter answered: "Thou art Christ, the Son of the living God."

Then Jesus continued saying: "Thou art Peter and upon this rock I will build my church, and the gates of hell shall not prevail against it. And I will give you the keys of the kingdom of heaven; and whatever thou shalt bind on earth shall be bound in heaven, and whatever thou shalt loose on earth shall be loosed in heaven."

Peter's office was thereby clearly defined. He was to be the chief steward of this house, and he would dictate the laws of the house.

Christ, in the Holy Eucharist, found in the church established by Peter is the spiritual bread from heaven. This was to come in the Last Supper, just before the Jews captured Jesus, who was to be condemned to death.

Jesus had now definitely proclaimed his messiahship, but only his disciples knew about it. He told the Apostles to tell no one that he was Jesus the Christ.

So from then on Jesus began to show his apostles that he must go to Jerusalem and suffer many things from the elders and scribes and chief priests, and be put to death, and on the third day rise again.

The sharp warning was a hard blow for his apostles. And Peter, who was generous both by nature and from the new office of steward of Christ's church on earth, felt he must say something about all of this.

And Peter said to Jesus: "Far be it from thee O Lord, this will never happen to thee."

Jesus turned to Peter and said: "Get behind me. Thou art a scandal to me, for you do not mind the things of God, but those of men."

Christ rebuked Peter because of the lingering desire in the minds of Peter and the other apostles for a *conquering Messiah* and a reluctance to accept the *suffering Messiah* instead. Since Peter was their leader, appointed by Jesus as steward of his church which was to be established, it was necessary to correct Peter in his concept about Christ's mission and death on the cross. The other apostles still had to realize the truth about Christ's death on the cross. The apostles still dreamed of a life of magnificence with Jesus on earth as a conqueror.

But Jesus shattered these dreams by telling them that those who would follow him must take up their cross. Even the apostles now realized that Jesus would die on the cross. Anyone who wanted to follow Jesus had to consider himself already dead; only then would he live.

By losing his life to the cause of Jesus and "good tidings" he would be saved, but if he remained desperately attached to his life, he would lose it. In fact, how does it profit a man to gain the whole world, if he loses his soul by failing to gain life eternal?

For Jesus, the present life is transitory and has value only so far as it is directed to the enduring life of the future. He, the Messiah, guides men toward the harsh trials of our imperfect existence. Whoever does not follow Jesus, choosing instead this transient life, chooses death.

Again Jesus went alone with his disciples and warned them

again about his death: "The Son of man is to be betrayed into the hands of men, and they will kill him; and on the third day he will rise again."

This warning was very necessary because the disciples did not fully understand all that Jesus was telling them.

The enemies of Jesus were following him around, trying to get a chance to sieze him for arrest. Since Jesus told them right out he was sent from heaven, these adversaries ran to the temple to see if they could not arrange for his arrest on charges of blasphemy. But his time had not yet come, and no one succeeded in laying their hands upon him. His enemies were well counterbalanced by his enthusiastic admirers.

When Jesus told his listeners again in the temple: "If I glorify myself, my glory is nothing. It is my Father who glorifies me, of whom you say that he is your God. And you do not know him, but I know him. And if I say I do not know him I shall be like you, a liar. Abraham, your father, rejoiced that he was to see my day. He saw it and was glad."

The Jews therefore said to him: "Thou are not yet fifty years old and hast thou seen Abraham?"

Jesus said to them: "Amen, Amen, I say to you, before Abraham came to be I am."

The discussion ended. Jesus had proclaimed that he was before Abraham and therefore before all Hebraism. Either they had to believe in Jesus or else follow the Hebrew Law and call him a blasphemer. According to Hebrew Law a blasphemer must be stoned. Therefore, they took up stones to cast at Jesus, but he hid himself and went out of the temple.

And so Jesus went on with his preaching and his miracles, and the scribes and the Pharisees kept right after him.

In their pursuit, they had an adulteress dragged to Jesus. They could not trap Jesus into saying he had broken the law in setting this woman free. Jesus would not answer their questions but told them: "Let him who is without sin, cast the first stone."

No one answered Jesus, and he told this woman: "Has no one condemned thee?" She said: "No one Lord." Jesus said: "Neither will I then, go and sin no more."

There were more of these incidents where the Pharisees were trying to get Jesus, but his time had not yet come.

One of his miracles was the healing of the blind beggar near the temple. One Sabbath, Jesus passed a blind man who was begging alms. Seeing this, the disciples with Jesus asked: "Rabbi, who has sinned, this man or his parents, that he should be born blind?" This question by the disciples was based on the old Hebrew notion that every physical ill was a consequence of some wrongdoing.

Jesus rejected this idea, saying that neither the man nor his parents had sinned, and this case had been permitted so that the works of God might be made known. Jesus then said: "As long as I am in the world, I am the light of the world."

When Jesus said this, he spat on the ground and with his spittle made a little clay, then he spread the clay over the blind man's eyes. Then Jesus said to the man: "Go wash yourself in the pool of Siloe." And the man went and washed, and when he returned, he could see.

The inevitable discussions followed this miracle because the man was well known as a professional beggar, and very well known throughout the city as a person blind from birth. When questioned, the man himself replied: "It is no one else. I am the beggar who was born blind." And he told them how Jesus performed the miracle. Then they wanted to ask Jesus about this, but he was gone.

This matter was serious because of the miracle and because Jesus had done this on the Sabbath. So this man was brought before the Pharisees, who asked the same questions and got the same answers.

The Pharisees declared: "This man is not of God because he does not observe the Sabbath." But others said: "If this man is a sinner how can he perform miracles like this?"

It was certain the blind man was cured; but it was even more certain that whoever made a fingerful of clay on the Sabbath was a sinner, and therefore could not work miracles. There was no escape from the dilemma.

This beggar was considered a sinner according to the Pharisees. They also considered Jesus a sinner. They continued to question the beggar and finally he began to lose his patience and said: "I have already told you all I know. Why do you want to hear it again? Do you too perchance want to become disciples of Jesus?"

A deluge of curses and insults came from the Pharisees on the man who dared ask that sarcastic question. They declared: "You are that fellow's disciple, and we are the disciples of Moses. We know that God spoke to Moses, but as for this man Jesus, we do not know where he is from."

But the beggar stood his ground and replied: "Well, that is exactly what seems so strange, that you do not know where Jesus is from, when he has opened my eyes. It is very certain that God listens, not to sinners but to just and pious men; since the beginning of the world no one has opened the eyes of a man born blind. Now if this man were not from God, he could not have cured my eyes."

The Pharisees were stunned by these words. Who was this man, a blind beggar, who was begotten in sin as his blindness proved? How dare he try to teach the outstanding representatives of Hebrew "tradition" and learning? So they threw the beggar out.

Shortly after that, the beggar met Jesus, who said to him: "Do you believe in the Son of Man?"

The man answered: "Who is he Lord, that I may believe in Him?" Jesus replied: "Thou hast seen him (referring to the cure) and he it is who speaks to you."

Then the man exclaimed: "I believe Lord," and falling down, he worshipped Jesus.

Jesus added: "For judgment have I come into this world, that they who do not see may see, and they who see, become blind."

At this time, some Pharisees came and overheard these last words of Jesus. They felt these words referred to themselves. The Pharisees asked Jesus: "Are we also blind?" He answered: "If you were only blind, you would have no sin. But now that you say we see, your sin remains."

In other words, blindness is a general condition, but it can be cured only if one recognizes that he is afflicted with it. Anyone who deludes himself that he can see will never be cured.

Jesus spoke of the coming of the Son of Man: "You must be ready, because at that hour, that you do not expect, the Son of Man is coming."

What is the "coming" of the Son of Man? *It is the coming that will manifest the eternal and unchanging consequences of Jesus' teaching.*

Jesus had spoken of renouncing riches, choosing instead, treasure in heaven. Riches must be renounced and the present world viewed as something fleeting, precisely because of the "coming" of the Son of Man.

The "coming" of the Son of Man shall dispel the shadow and reveal the abiding substance, melt away the accumulated riches of earth, distribute the invisible treasure of heaven, fill the expectations of those who have hoped for that "coming," and establish, in eternity, their lot of blessedness.

Jesus kept right on with his teaching and his miracles, even though the Pharisees were still trying to capture him and put him to death. At Bethany they ordered his arrest and were only a short distance away. After the order for his arrest had been given, Jesus disappeared.

Jesus resurrected Lazarus from the dead, even after four days, when Lazarus was already buried in his tomb. This caused quite a lot of excitement among the people.

Of course, the Pharisees knew about it, and being very anxious, they turned to the high priests. A council was called and the question was asked: "What are we doing for this man is working many signs. If we let him alone, all will believe in Him, and the Romans will come and take away both our Temple and our nation."

They did not discuss the reality of Jesus' miracles, nor did they discuss Jesus himself at all. The Roman masters of Palestine were beginning to be annoyed by the interminable procession of subversive wonder-workers that had been cropping up for a long time, and perhaps this "Jesus" would be the one to provoke the extreme severity that would end the procession forever. It was easy to foresee what would happen. Jesus would continue to work his miracles; the people would flock to him and proclaim him King of Israel. The Roman cohorts stationed in Palestine and eventually the legions of Syria would fall upon the rebels; the result would be first a massacre of the Jews and then the destruction of the "holy" place and next the destruction of the entire nation. The danger was grave and some plan had to be decided upon immediately.

Caiphas, then high priest, after listening awhile to various plans, expressed his opinion with all the imperviousness permitted by his office: "You know nothing at all; nor do you reflect that it is expedient for us that one man die for the people, instead of the whole nation perishing." Caiphas had not named anyone, but they all understood; the "one man" to die "for the nation" was Jesus. True, he was not inciting the people nor had he ever paid any attention whatever to matters political; true he was innocent, as some of those present had just pointed out. But what did that matter? If he died, the whole nation would escape ruin, and that was reason enough for his death.

Caiphas, being high priest of the year, prophesied that Jesus was to die for the nation; also, he was to die so that he might gather into one the children of God who were scattered abroad.

So their plan from that day forth was to put Jesus to death.

Passion Week brought Jesus' triumphal entry into Jerusalem. This time, for sure, the people thought Jesus would be made King of the Jews and he would take over as an earthly King. They knew they would be safe with Jesus as their King on earth.

After they arrived at Jerusalem, Jesus said to two of his apostles: "The hour has come for the Son of Man to be glorified. Amen, Amen, I say to you, unless the grain of wheat fall into the ground and die, it remains alone. But if it die, it brings forth much fruit."

Here again is the concept of the *glorification of death;* the kingdom of God will be completely diffused in the manner destined for it in the present "world" only after its founder has been destroyed like the grain of wheat buried in the damp earth.

Jesus was asked which was the greatest commandment of all, and he answered: "The Lord our God is one God; and thou shalt love the Lord thy God with your whole heart, and with your whole soul, and with your whole mind, and with your whole strength."

The second commandment is similar: "Thou shalt love thy neighbor as thyself."

Jeus said there were no commandments greater than these two.

It is well to note here that according to the Rabbis, the written Law, or Torah, contained *613* precepts, *248* of which were commandments, while *365* were prohibitions.

Both commands and prohibitions were divided into two groups, the light and the heavy, according to their importance.

The Last Supper

Jesus sent Peter and John into the city of Jerusalem to prepare for the Passover so Jesus could eat the Passover with his apostles. The preparations were completed during the day, and that night Jesus and his apostles gathered together to celebrate the Passover.

It was at this time Jesus told his apostles that one of them would betray him. Of course, this was Judas, who accepted thirty pieces of silver later to show the soldiers where Jesus was in the garden of olives.

After the usual Pascal meal was finished, Jesus completed the news he had given his followers and apostles. The time was close now for Jesus to be taken prisoner and then crucified.

Jesus took a flat round loaf of unleavened bread, and having said the blessing over it, he broke it in pieces, which he gave to the apostles, saying: "Take and eat; this is my body, which is being given for you; do this in remembrance of me."

A little while later, Jesus took a chalice of wine mixed with water, and having given thanks, he made them all drink of it saying: "All of you drink this. This cup is the new covenant in my blood, which is being shed for many. Do this as often as you drink it in remembrance of me."

The Last Supper certainly could only be the fulfillment of

the promise Jesus had made so many times during his public life on earth. In his teachings, Jesus had mentioned several times: "I am the living bread that has come down from heaven. If anyone eat of this bread, he shall have eternal life. He who eats my flesh and drinks my blood abides in me and I in him."

The Synoptics do not tell us just what impression these two acts made on the apostles personally. Much more important was the permanent impression they left on all of the first Christian society, which was, from every point of view, the most reliable interpreter of these two acts of Jesus and the words which accompanied them.

About twenty-five years after the Last Supper, Paul wrote to the Christians of Corinth, a letter in which he described the Eucharist as a permanent rite, in which the faithful who partook of it ate the real Body and drank the real Blood of Jesus, which was derived directly from Jesus' twofold act of consecration at the Last Supper and his death.

Forty years after the Epistle of Paul, we find the apostle John, who places special emphasis on its spiritual effects in the discourse on the "Bread of Life."

The eucharistic liturgy was established in every Christian community by the end of the fifth century.

At Jesus' "Last Discourses," he mentioned: "I will come to you. Yet a little while and the world will no longer see me. But you see me, for I live and you shall live. He who has my commandments *and keeps them,* he it is who loves me."

Jesus also said: "Peace I leave with you, my peace I give to you; not as the world gives do I give it to you. Do not let your heart be troubled, or be afraid."

The arrest of Jesus followed.

Judas, one of the apostles, came to the garden where Jesus was praying. With Judas was a crowd of people and soldiers with swords and clubs, sent from the chief priests and elders of the people and also from the Roman procurator. Jesus was arrested and taken prisoner.

Next, Jesus was taken to the house of the high priest, Annas, that same night. They questioned Jesus but the trial lasted only a short time.

Early the next morning, Jesus was again taken on trial. This time they accused Jesus of blasphemy because he answered "yes" when the accusers asked him: "Are you the Son of God?"

They condemned Jesus to death.

After the trial, Jesus was turned over to the Roman soldiers, who placed a crown of thorns on Jesus head and called him King of the Jews. They kicked him and beat him until he was bleeding. So Jesus took this terrible abuse from weak, ignorant, and vicious human beings, until he was taken before Pilate and Herod.

During this time the apostles of Jesus were around the courtyard watching the proceedings. However, they fled in terror when they were discovered. Only Peter stayed, and he denied he ever knew Jesus. After that, he went away and wept bitterly.

When Jesus was taken before Pilate, the Roman official asked the crowd outside what they were accusing Jesus of. They answered: "If he were not a criminal we would not have handed him over to you."

Pilate did not want to get involved with the Jews on questions of religion, so he said: "Take this man yourselves, and judge him according to your law."

But it was not lawful for them to put anyone to death. Pilate understood that the accusers wanted the prisoner put to death, but they were powerless to do it.

Thus Jesus' case was presented before the civil authority. But proofs were necessary to convince the new judge—Pilate. He did not know about Jesus.

The Jews then said to him: "We have found this man perverting our nation, and forbidding the payment of taxes to Caesar, and saying that he is 'Christ a King.' This was strictly a political charge and took the place of the religious charges against Jesus which stated that he was a blasphemer when he said he was the Son of God in heaven.

Thus Pilate, as a man of law, was determined to expose the duplicity of the accusers; but as a Roman magistrate, he was the guardian of the Roman authority. There was nothing to do but question Jesus.

So Pilate asked Jesus: "Are you King of the Jews?"

Jesus answered: "Do you say this of yourself, or have others told it to you?"

Pilate was annoyed by this question from Jesus and said: "Am I a Jew? Thy own people and high priests have delivered you to me. What have you done?"

Jesus' answer again distinguished between two meanings in Pilate's original question: "My Kingdom is not of this world. If my Kingdom was of this world, my followers would have fought that I might not be delivered to the Jews. But, as it is, my Kingdom is not from here."

Pilate, determined to clarify one point at least, said: "Thou art then a King."

Jesus said he was truly a King. "This is why I was born, and why I have come into the world, to bear witness to the truth. Everyone who is of the truth hears my voice."

The crowd outside was noisy, making accusations.

He asked Jesus: "Do you have no answer to make?" But Jesus made no answer.

He went outside and told the crowd: "I find no guilt in this man." This should have ended the trial then and there. The Sanhedrists were furious and protested violently, all shouting against Jesus at one time. They said: "Jesus is stirring up the people, teaching throughout all Judea, and beginning from Galilee even to this place."

These last words caught Pilate's attention because they seemed to offer a solution to the problem. This gave Pilate a chance to send Jesus to the jurisdiction of Herod.

Herod questioned Jesus but finally sent him back to Pilate because he found no guilt in Jesus.

Pilate proceeded to offer the accusers another consoling solution. During the Pasch, it was the custom for the procurator to release some prisoner at the request of the multitude. Thus it seemed to Pilate that it would be right and convenient at this time to grant Jesus the favor, for justice would be saved at least in part and the accusers would be satisfied as well.

There was in prison at the time a notorious malefactor called Barabbas. Pilate thought, given the choice between Jesus and Barabbas, the accusers would certainly ask for Jesus. So he went to the threshold of the praetorium and said: "Whom do you wish that I release to you? Barabbas, or Jesus, who is called Christ, King of the Jews?"

The crowd was persuaded by the chief priests and the elders to cry: "Give us Barabbas and destroy Jesus."

Pilate asked them: "Why, What evil has he done?" He shouted: "I am innocent of the blood of this man, look you to it."

Finally, the crowd won over Pilate and Jesus was scourged and condemned to death. The effect was mob hysteria. People just panicked and lost their reasoning power.

After the terrible scourging and abuse of Jesus by the soldiers, he was unable to carry his heavy cross.

A man named Simon of Cyrene happened to be passing by. The centurion ordered Simon to help Jesus carry his cross.

There were a group of women, "daughters of Jerusalem," following Jesus and weeping to see him treated so cruelly.

Jesus returned their compassion when he said: "Weep not for me but for your children."

When the procession of Jesus and the two common thieves reached the place called Skull, the crucifixion was carried out at once. All three were stripped of their garments, though they may have been given some kind of loin cloth.

So far as it is known, Jesus said nothing while he was nailed to the cross. There was hardly any strength left in his body. Presently, he prayed aloud to his Father in Heaven: "Father forgive them for they know not what they do." Jesus was asking pardon from God for the people who had condemned him to death.

It would seem that Judas, who had betrayed Jesus, would receive his prayer for pardon. Judas was sorry for his wrongdoing afterwards and tried to take the silver pieces back to the Pharisees.

Jesus was hanging on the cross, and the chief priests and other Sanhedrists were on the ground below him. They still taunted Jesus: "You who destroyed the Temple and in three days built it up again, save yourself. If you are the Son of God, come down from the cross."

Others said: "He saved others; himself he cannot save! If he is the King of Israel, let him come down now from the cross, and we will believe him. He trusted in God. Let God deliver him now, if he wants him; for he said: 'I am the Son of God.'" But Jesus did not answer them.

Also, there were insults and reproaches from the two thieves beside Jesus. One of the thieves asked Jesus: "If you are Christ the Messiah, save thyself and us."

But the other robber rebuked the first one saying: "Do you not even fear God, seeing that you are under the same sentence? And we indeed suffer justly for we are receiving what our deeds deserved; but this man has done nothing wrong."

This thief knew Jesus by his reputation. In spite of his crimes, this man had some good in him. Turning to Jesus he said: "Lord remember me when you come into your kingdom. When you come reigning gloriously in that Kingdom which you have foretold."

And Jesus answered the thief: "Amen I say to thee, this day you shall be with me in paradise."

Mary, the mother of Jesus, was standing near the cross with Jesus on it, and John, the beloved apostle of Jesus, also was there. Jesus said to Mary: "Woman behold thy son," and then to John he said: "Behold thy mother." From that day on, John took Mary, the mother of Jesus, into his house.

Jesus was failing rapidly on the cross, and suddenly he cried aloud: "My God, my God, why hast thou forsaken me?" Hence, Jesus once more asserted that he was the Messiah.

When Jesus said: "I thirst," the soldiers offered him vinegar and water.

Then Jesus murmured: "It is consummated. Then he cried out: "Father, into your hands I commend my spirit." Then Jesus bowed his head and died.

The sky darkened and there were earthquake tremors at this time. The soldiers were afraid and said: "This truly was a just man."

The Sanhedrists remembered a precept of the law, that Jesus' body must be buried that same afternoon before sunset. This would make the *murder of Jesus* a *holy deed*. The soldiers took the body of Jesus down from the cross for burial.

Nicodemus was there with a mixture of myrrh and aloes. Joseph brought the shroud to cover Jesus' body. Joseph had a tomb of his own. He let them place the body of Jesus in it for burial. Thus Jesus was buried, and a great stone rolled in front of the tomb.

Mary Magdalene and the other Mary prepared spices and ointments for Jesus' body. That Galilean Rabbi was actually gone; he was safely dead. There was no danger that they would ever have to listen to his invectives again and be humiliated in the eyes of the people. His disciples would scatter now that their master was dead.

Then they remembered that Jesus had told them he would rise from the dead in three days. So they went to Pilate and told him: "Sir, we have remembered how that deceiver said, while he was alive: 'After three days I will rise again.' Give orders therefore, that the sepulcher be guarded until the third day, or else his disciples may come and steal him away, and say to the people: 'He has risen from the dead; and the last imposture will be worse than the first!'

Pilate told them: "You have a guard; go and guard it as well as you know how."

The Jewish leaders, being very suspicious, went and sealed the tomb so no one could enter without breaking the seal.

The same historical documents which have narrated the story of Jesus up to this point do not stop with his death, but with the same authority they relate his resurrection and second life.

No one saw Jesus in the act of rising from the dead. But his resurrection was accompanied by extraordinary signs: "And behold there was a great earthquake; for an angel of the Lord came down from heaven, and rolled the stone back and sat upon it. But the tomb was empty."

All four apostles agreed that the sepulcher was empty early Sunday morning. The soldiers guarding the tomb woke up and all these things terrified them and they ran for safety outside the city gate.

The women who prepared Jesus' body for burial returned very early in the morning. Mary Magdalene rushed to the tomb and found it empty. The tomb was open, and the body of Jesus was gone. The soldiers had fled in terror and Mary Magdalene didn't know what had happened.

The women returned to Jerusalem and found the apostles and told them about Jesus' disappearance, but they could not believe it. Peter and John came back to the tomb to find out for themselves. They found the linen laying there that had been wrapped around the body of Jesus. And they knew the body had not been stolen.

Later, Jesus appeared to Mary Magdalene. He told her to tell the apostles that she had seen Jesus alive. She told them but they would not believe her. Other people had not yet heard about Jesus' appearing to Mary Magdalene.

Two of Jesus' disciples were walking down the road to Emmaus, where they lived. One was named Cleophas. Hopeless and dispirited by the crucifixion, death, and burial of Jesus, these two apostles were talking about the events. As they walked along, talking and arguing, Jesus himself appeared and drew near them, walking along with them. The disciples did not notice it was Jesus, and he asked them: "What words are you exchanging as you walk?"

They wondered who this stranger was to question them like that. Cleophas answered Jesus: "Are you the only stranger in Jerusalem who does not know the things that have happened in these days?" Jesus said: "What things?" And they said to him: "Concerning Jesus of Nazareth, who was a prophet, mighty in work and word before God and all the people; and how our high priests and rulers delivered him up to be sentenced to death, and crucified him. But we were hoping it would be he who would redeem Israel." They meant that Jesus would redeem the holy people from all foreign domination, but this hope disappeared with his death.

Cleophas continued: "Besides all of this today is the third day after his death. Moreover certain women, who were at the tomb, astounded us by saying they had seen a vision of angels, who said he is alive, but they did not see him."

These words show that these two disciples left Jerusalem before it was known that Jesus appeared to Mary Magdalene.

Jesus said to them: "Did not Jesus have to suffer these things before entering into his glory?"

After they arrived where the two disciples lived, they asked Jesus (the stranger) to stay with them because it was towards evening. And it came to pass that Jesus reclined at the table with them. Jesus took the bread and blessed it and he began handing it to them. At this time they recognized Jesus and he vanished from their sight.

The two disciples were so excited about this that they returned at once to Jerusalem and found the eleven apostles gathered together. They were saying: "The Lord has risen indeed, and has appeared to Simon." The apostles were hiding in fear of the Jews, but they had found a safe place.

On that same day, Jesus had appeared to Simon Peter, Mary Magdalene, and the two disciples and blessed them and broke bread with them.

While they were discussing these things, Jesus himself appeared and stood in their midst, saying to them: "Peace be to you." But they were terrified and thought they were seeing a spirit. So Jesus said: "Why are you troubled? And why do doubts arise in your hearts? See my hands and feet, that is my very self. Feel me and see; for a spirit hath not flesh and bones, as you see me to have." Saying this, Jesus showed them his hands and his feet.

Jesus asked them if they had any food to eat. They handed him part of a broiled fish and he ate it. Then Jesus said: "As the Father has sent me, so I also send you. Receive the Holy Spirit; whose sins you shall retain, they are retained."

The old promise made the apostles regarding the future government of the church was hereby fulfilled.

Thomas was not at this meeting. He had said he would not believe it was Jesus unless he could put his hand into his side and see the print of the nails in his hands.

After eight days, the apostles were again gathered together inside, and Thomas was with them. Jesus appeared and stood in their midst, saying: "Peace be to you." Then he said to Thomas: "Bring here thy finger, and see my hands, and bring thy hand and put it into my side."

Thomas answered and said to him: "My Lord and My God." Jesus said to him: "Because you have seen, you have believed. Blessed are those who have not seen and yet have believed."

All these appearances of Jesus took place in Jerusalem or nearby Judea. There were other appearances in Galilee, where the apostles went after the Pasch was ended.

One evening Peter and the rest of the apostles went fishing. They went out in their boat, but the fishing was poor and they had caught nothing. When they were near the shore on their return to land, they glimpsed a figure through the mist; it seemed to be a man waiting for them. When they were within calling distance, he asked: "Young men, have you any fish?" They answered no, but the man shouted again: "Cast the net to the right of the boat and you will find them."

Who was this unknown man giving them such confident advice? Anyway, it was worth one more cast where the man had indicated, *and now they were unable to draw it up because of the great number of fish*. At this the apostles remembered what had happened before. John recognized Jesus standing on the shore, and shouted: "It is the Lord."

Peter swam to the shore, and the others came in slowly with the boat. When they disembarked, they saw a little fire already lit. Jesus told them to bring some of the fish they had just caught. There were about 150 large fish.

The apostles had a breakfast of fish and bread with Jesus.

They wanted to ask him many questions but were afraid. Jesus said to Peter: "Do you love me?" and Peter said: "Lord thou knowest all things, thou knowest that I love you." Jesus replied: "Feed my sheep."

This question pertained to the day of Caesarea Philippi, when Jesus had proclaimed Peter as the rock which was the foundation of the church and had charged Peter to govern it as a shepherd rules his flock.

Peter had to remember that this office was to be a labor of love, a consequence of the love he professed for Jesus. The supreme shepherd would depart from his flock, but he would not leave it unprotected. In his place, Jesus left a shepherd who was his vicar and who must rule it with the same love and for the same love which had animated the supreme Shepherd.

Jesus predicted the death of Peter, just as it later happened. They put Peter in chains and led him to his execution as they had Jesus. Peter was killed because of his faith in Jesus and his love of the office entrusted to him by Jesus.

Later, Jesus met the apostles in a mountain, where he told them: "All power in Heaven and on earth has been given to me. Go therefore and make disciples of all nations, baptizing them in the name of the Father, and of the Son, and of the Holy Spirit, teaching them to observe all that I have commanded you. *And behold I am with you all days even unto the consummation of the world.*"

The church founded by Jesus was now entering a new period which is to last until the end of the world.

The duty of the new disciples will be to observe what Jesus has commanded his first disciples to observe.

Above all, the Shepherd (Jesus) Himself Will Help And Protect His Flock, In An Invisible But No Less Effective Manner. He Will Be Among His Future Disciples, "Even Unto the Consummation of the World." Here, therefore, ends the story of Jesus and the story of the church begins: the life of Christ "according to the flesh" comes to a close, and the "mystical" Christ begins.

There has been nothing said about the appearance of Christ in his physical body. The Ascension occurred on the Mount of Olives near Bethany, forty days after the Resurrection. At this time his followers still wanted Jesus to restore the kingdom of Israel, even though Jesus had told them so many times: "My Kingdom is not of this earth, but in Heaven with God."

X

The Supernatural Help Provided by Christ for Nearly 2,000 Years

In order to understand the whole perspective of what God expects from his people, we certainly must understand that God has planned nothing but *good* for all of us. Therefore, we can understand that God is not just waiting, as a supernatural being somewhere unknown, for us to make a human mistake and then punish us some way or other. Maybe we don't even know when or how.

When people believed, as they have down through the centuries, that the first man and woman made God terribly angry because they ate apples from a tree God had forbidden, there had to be a time when God would let them know the truth about what he really expected them to do as people on earth.

For many centuries people believed that God had driven our first ancestors out of paradise. They were tempted by a snake, who was supposed to be Satan himself, the supreme devil, who revolted against God and was driven out of heaven and into hell forever; they were told they would be like God himself if they ate the apples from this one tree.

In his great anger, God was supposed to have condemned the first man and woman to a life of suffering and finally death. They could have stayed in the Garden of Paradise without work or suffering. They would have lived there forever.

So they committed this great sin against God and had to be punished for it. They would have to die because of this, instead of having Heaven here on earth.

Even worse, every single person born on this earth after them would be punished the same way for the *first sin* of the first man and woman. Every human being was blamed for this first sin. Because of this, we were all *born in sin.*

As the centuries went by, there were prophets who occasionally predicted that God would send a *Redeemer* to free all the people on earth from this great punishment.

There was one race who were called "the chosen people of God." It was through these people that the human race would be redeemed. A Savior would come to these people from God.

So it was easy for these people to be interested in John the Baptist when he came to earth as a man and a prophet. John was a very simple person who apparently lived on locusts and honey. He wore no clothes but a goat-skin loin cloth.

In his public appearances and his teaching, John went in exactly the opposite direction from what other prophets had predicted about the Messiah or Savior. John promised no kingdoms or supremacy, nor did he appeal to the use of force or armed weapons. John ignored all political matters. He worked no miracles. He had no earthly possessions.

The one message he taught was a *moral admonition.* He told people: "The Kingdom of God is imminent, *hence change your way of thinking.*"

The very first word of his proclamation was *REPENT.* This meant a complete transformation of the mind. Change your way of thinking.

Next, John told them: *"Confess Your Sins."* He meant by these words that people must make a public act to prove they had changed their way of thinking.

Thus, Baptism by John the Baptist meant: DEMON-STRATE IN PUBLIC THAT YOU HAD CHANGED YOUR MIND ABOUT SEEKING THE THINGS OF THE WORLD—AND YOU WILL SEEK THE SPIRITUAL KINGDOM OF GOD.

This was certainly not Baptism for the remission of the original sin of the first man and woman created by God.

Also, it did not mean we could go to Heaven if we were Baptized with water to do away with Original Sin.

John the Baptist was trying to get people prepared for the coming of the Messiah.

This preparation (Baptism) was to get people to publicly state they changed their way of thinking so they could believe in the Spiritual Kingdom of God in Heaven.

The Kingdom of God is in Heaven not here on earth. So the message Jesus brought from God in Heaven to the people on earth was that the Kingdom of God was spiritual and was in Heaven—*not on earth.*

This certainly was not the story that God would send a redeemer, His only son, Jesus, so that Jesus could be tortured and put to death by his enemies. Jesus was to die because of our sins and the Original Sin passed on to every human being.

The death of Jesus by his crucifixion was to have appeased God and satisfied him. Now, without Original Sin, God's people could go to Heaven. All we have to do is die and we will go to Heaven. Certainly, we have to thank Jesus for all of this.

Thus, according to history, well-recorded by the apostles of Jesus and John the Baptist, the problem of people on earth is not the sin of the first woman and man. The real problem is that people must change their way of thinking and place their faith and trust in God and in his spiritual kingdom in Heaven. They must not seek an earthly kingdom and glory, instead of God and his kingdom in Heaven.

The people that condemned Jesus to death believed in the

God of viciousness and believed in their own earthly kingdom with all the power and glory they could get. They could not believe Jesus was the Son of God; also, they were afraid Jesus and his followers and the people would overthrow their government and destroy them so they killed Jesus.

Jesus himself told the people that the Pharisees would kill him and that in three days he would rise from the dead, thus proving to them he was truly from Heaven, a spiritual kingdom, and truly, he was the Son of God.

And that is exactly what happened.

Christ preached to the people that they *must* believe in the spiritual God in Heaven instead of living for earthly things and pleasures; if they did not have this change of mind, they could not get to Heaven after they died.

There was no mention of the story of Original Sin. Of course, the apostles of Jesus could only write about what actually happened during the public life of Jesus.

People have been so mistaken about the mission of Christ on earth; this, in brief, is what they believed:

1. God created the world.
2. God created Adam and Eve.
3. The devil (in the form of a snake) tempted Adam and Eve to eat the apples from the forbidden tree, so they would become like God.
4. God knew this and drove Adam and Eve out of Paradise where they would have lived forever.
5. God was so mad at them he made them work, have sickness, suffer, and die.
6. All of their descendants would be born in sin and suffer the same as Adam and Eve.
7. Finally, God would send a Savior to earth. His only Son, Jesus, would come to earth. He would have to be crucified and die on the cross because of our sins and the Original Sin we inherited from Adam and Eve and their sin of eating the apples.

8. Jesus was raised from the dead and went to Heaven.
9. Now God was satisfied after Jesus was put to death and suffered so much.
10. God was so pleased that he now opened Heaven to people when they died.
11. Now all people can go to Heaven. All we have to do is say we believe in Jesus. He is our redeemer and our Savior.

The people who murdered Jesus thought they could follow the law of Moses the way they wanted, just so the law favored them. They didn't have to believe in God the way Jesus told them.

It was revenge they wanted, not to forgive their enemies. Jesus told them forgive other people seven times, yes, seventy times seven. This meant forgive indefinitely. There is enough proof about God and Christ so that we can understand that through Jesus, God has given us the necessary knowledge of how he wants us to live according to his will.

Jesus has told us many times: "I am the bread of life. Unless you eat my body and drink my blood, you shall not have life eternal."

By his crucifixion and his resurrection from the dead, and by his supernatural appearances to his apostles after his resurrection, Christ proved to people that there is a life possible for human beings after the death of their bodies.

Christ arose from his dead body and soul because that was the only way he could prove he was the Son of God in Heaven. Christ had to appear as a human being after his death to prove he actually had come back to life again just as he had promised a number of times to his followers.

Christ said: "I am the spiritual bread from Heaven," while he was on his earthly mission. Also, Christ said: "I want you to eat my spiritual flesh and drink my spiritual blood."

There is nothing else this could possibly mean except the supernatural presence of Christ in the "Blessed Sacrament" or "Holy Eucharist" as we find it today in all Catholic churches. This has been true since Peter established the church for Christ nearly 2,000 years ago.

God, in his justice, cannot hold any person responsible if he does not *honestly* know about Jesus and the Holy Eucharist. Even then, every human being has a soul within him that lets him know there is a creator and a God somewhere that he must serve and be subject to; that is, every person who has the use of his mind.

Christ in the Holy Eucharist

Jesus established the Holy Eucharist at the Last Supper, before his death.

The Catholic Church was established by Christ when he declared Peter the head or steward of his Church on Earth. The apostles were to go out and teach all nations the same message Jesus had brought to the people while on earth.

John the Baptist preached the coming of Christ, and his Baptism was to prepare people to change their minds about earthly things and believe in a heavenly Kingdom of God exclusively.

So the Catholic church now has the celebration of Mass every day in most of the churches.

The Holy Eucharist is kept in the tabernacle in fulfillment of the plan of Jesus.

During the Mass the unleavened bread has been changed into the body of Jesus.

Since the people could not believe that Jesus could give them his own body and blood when he stood right in front of them, it certainly is not easy for people living today to believe this.

But the fact remains that Jesus did tell them: "I am the spiritual bread from Heaven. Unless you eat of my body and drink of my blood, you shall not have eternal life."

The most important reason for Christ coming to earth in any form is to help people understand about God and eternal life in Heaven. For that same reason he is actually present in the Blessed Sacrament in the Catholic churches all over the world.

It is not hard to understand that we all need help, every day of our lives. The help we need just cannot be received from any human being on earth. It has to come from a supernatural source. Christ is the supernatural means we have on earth in the Blessed Sacrament. Christ will never fail to help any human being who goes to the church to visit him in the Blessed Sacrament.

Of course, a person must be sincere in asking the help of Jesus. A person must submit his will to the will of Jesus and God.

People must realize that Christ is present in the Holy Eucharist, just as he promised the apostles and others on earth.

The supernatural help of Christ is there if people want to go to his church and visit him.

XI

To Get the Most Out of Life
People Must Choose Supernatural Help

In review, let us go back and remember that a supernatural power has created the universe and all the rest of the beings, including the people on earth.

Since the life on earth of a human being is only limited to a few years, at the most, God did not plan for people to live here forever. Because of this short life here, people must live so that there is a possibility of life after death. The only way a person can live for a future existence is to turn his mind to God our Creator and accept whatever he wants to give us.

People have no choice but to accept what God has planned for them on earth. This choice of God, above everything else, must come of their own free will, and it must come while they are alive and have use of their reasoning power.

The building of a person's character, as previously discussed, is in accordance with Christ's explanation to his followers on earth and according to good judgment on the part of each individual.

To maintain our bodies in good condition is the foundation of good health during our life on earth. God meant for us to learn to eat the foods he provided for us, not to have people change his food to suit them the way they wanted it.

Nature and good books are now available to tell people what foods to eat and how to prepare them so the best food can be received for our bodies to keep us healthy. Our conscience and our mind lets us know when we have been trying to live the best way.

When we try to be fair and honest with our neighbors and our conscience according to God's plan, we know we have done the right thing. As a result, we are satisfied mentally and feel well repaid for our actions.

When we try to follow God in our day-by-day living, our soul is given the help to keep us on the right way to life everlasting, with God and Christ in Heaven.

Our bodies help us get through this life on earth. Our souls are carried on into a spiritual life in the Kingdom of God in Heaven; that is, if we follow Jesus, who told us the greatest commandment of God: "The Lord Our God Is One God. And We Must Love God With Our Whole Mind, With Our Whole Body, With Our Whole Heart, And With Our Whole Strength."

Each person holds the final choice as to how he wants to live his life. He shall live and believe as he so chooses. But right or wrong, he must accept the final reward for the way he choses to live his life on earth.

The information about the Life of Christ in this book can be found in: *Life of Christ* by Giuseppe Ricciotti, The Bruce Publishing Company, 1947.